SYDNEY'S BIRTHDAY COLORING BOOK

KIDS PERSONALIZED BOOKS

Can't Find Your Name?

Have our elves create a personalized book
with the name of your choice today!

VISIT US AT:

PERSONALIZETHISBOOK.COM

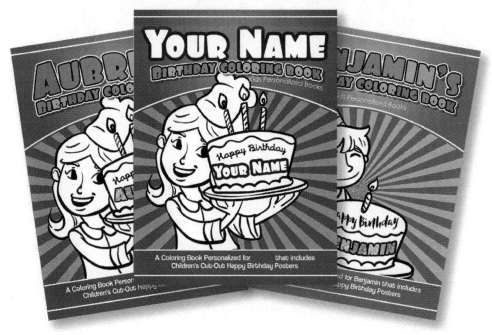

Chiquita publishing

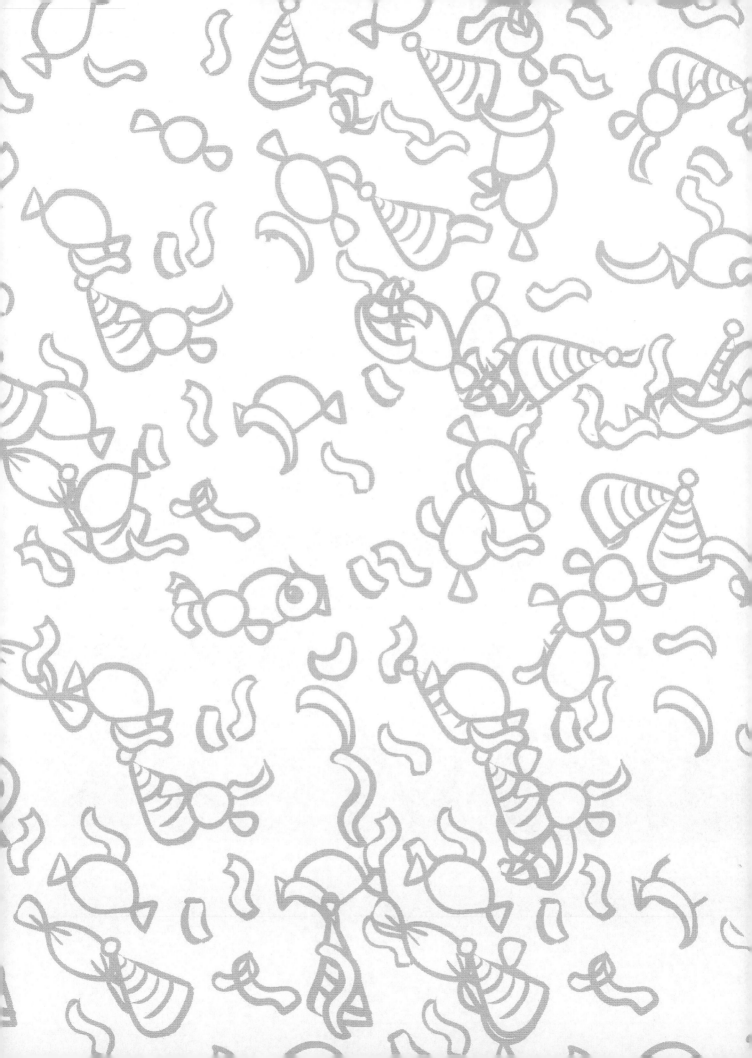

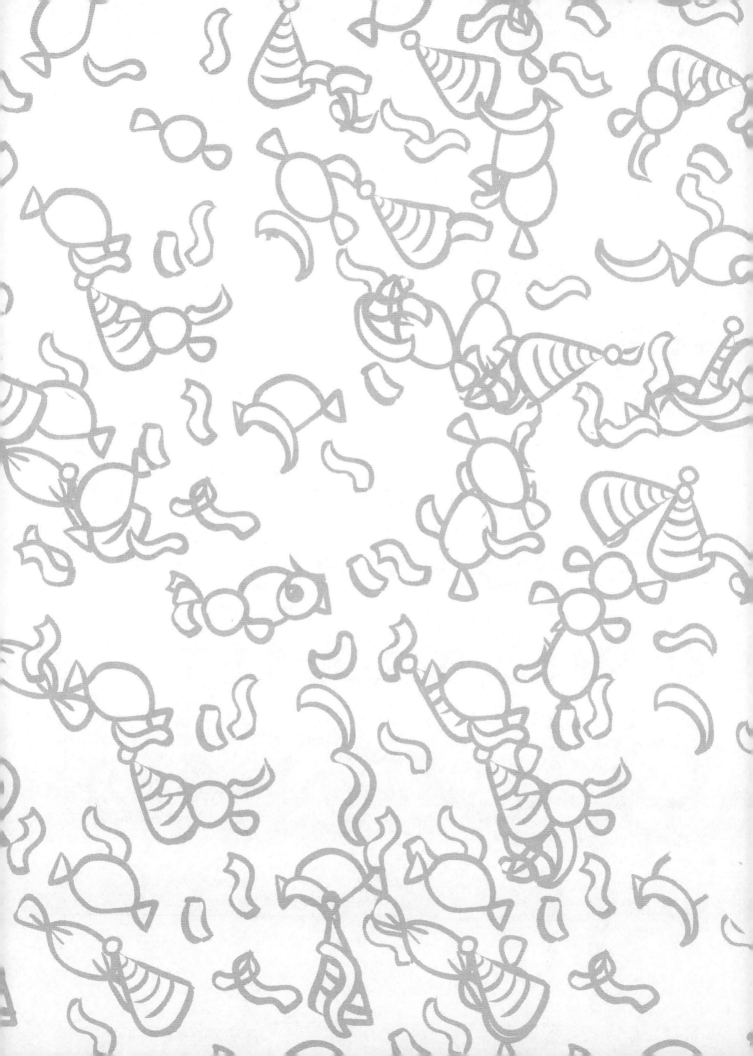

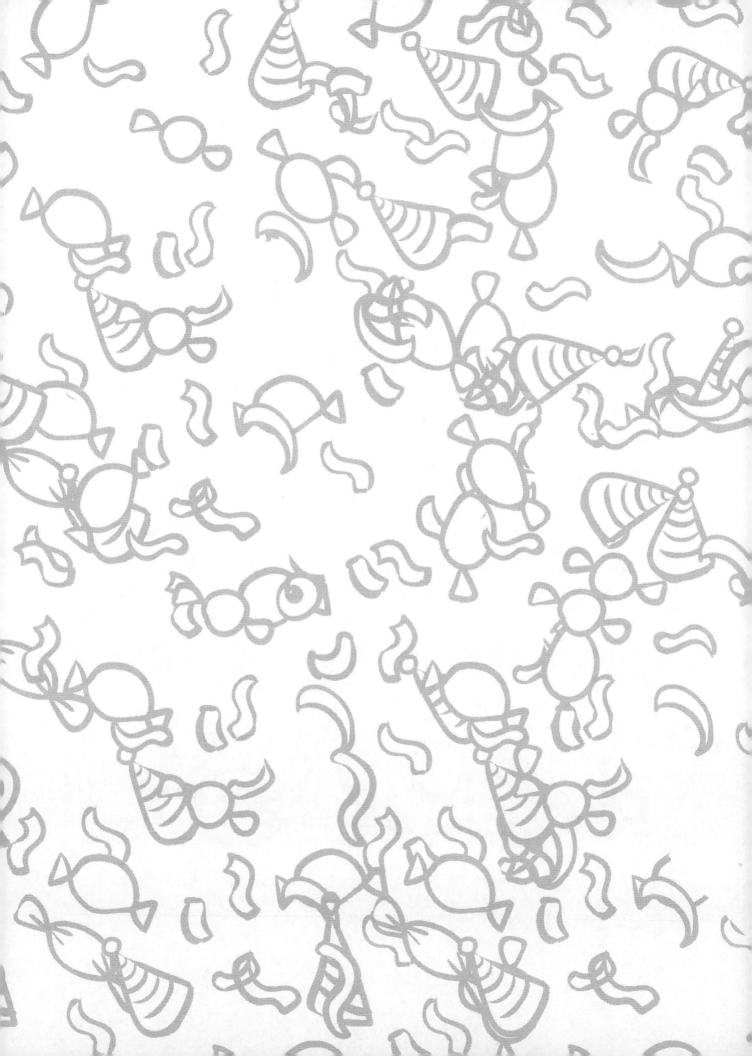

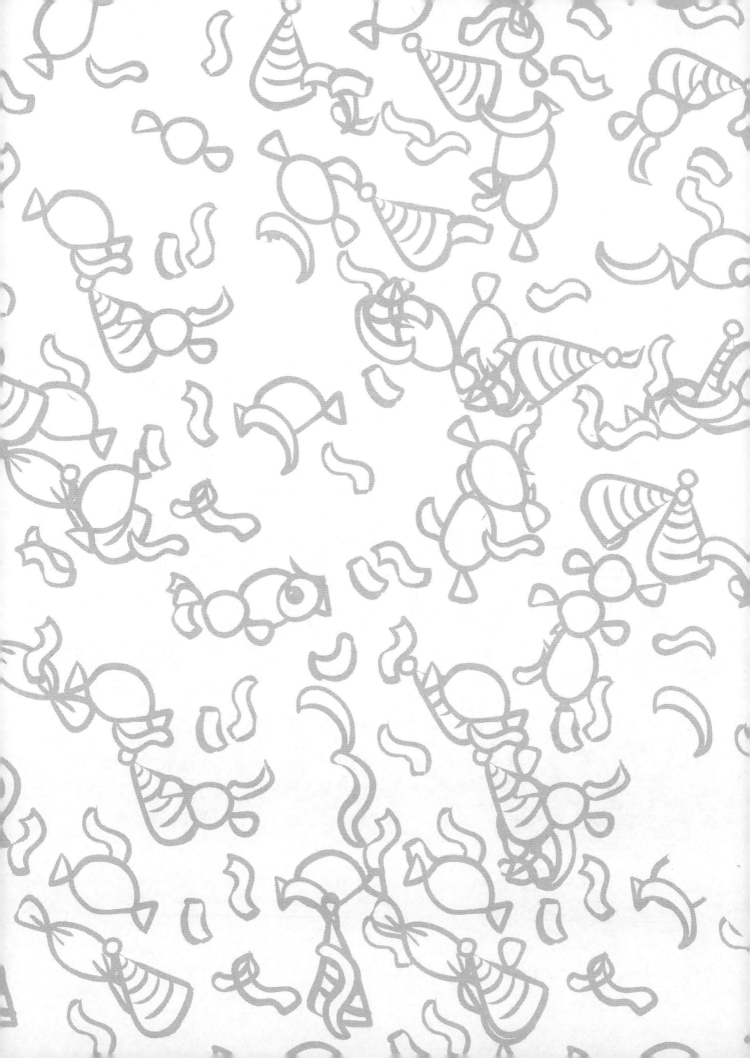

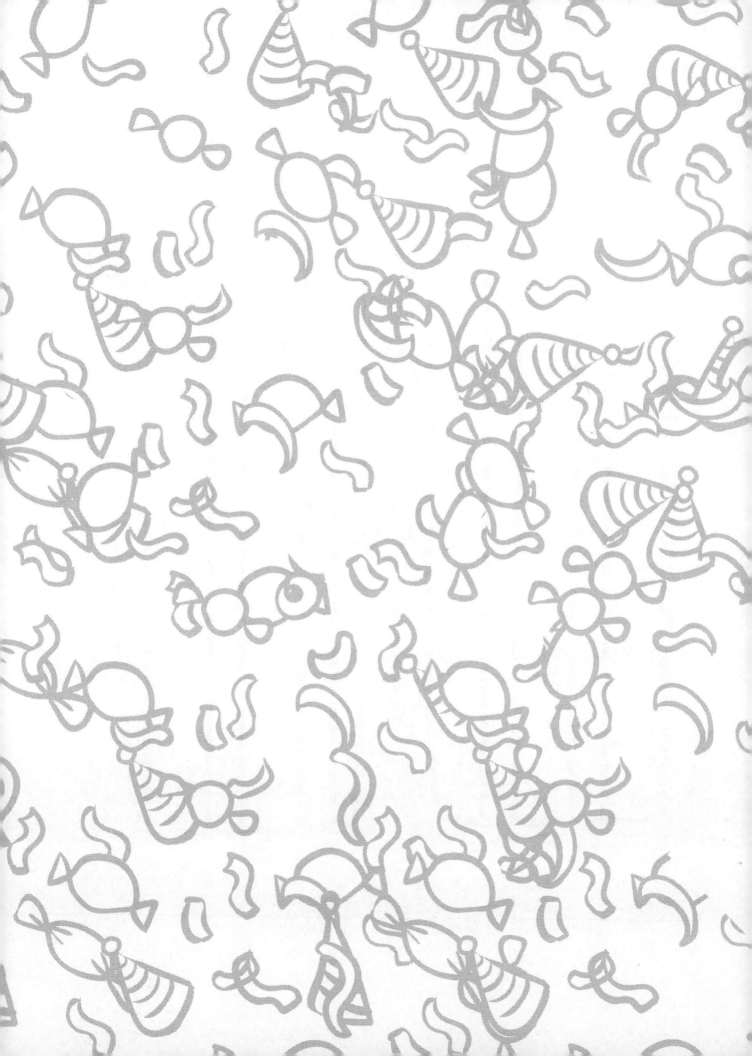

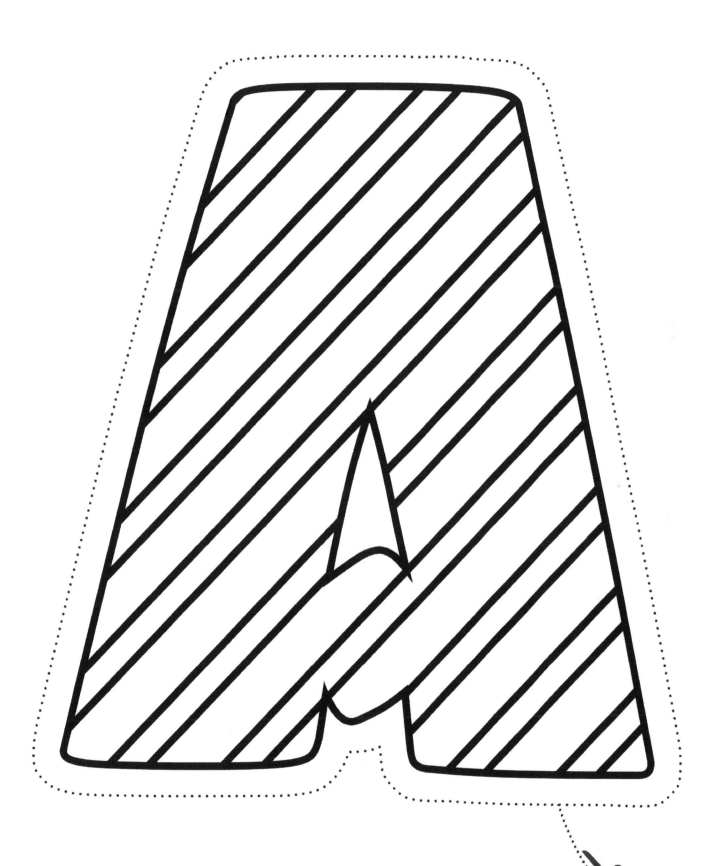

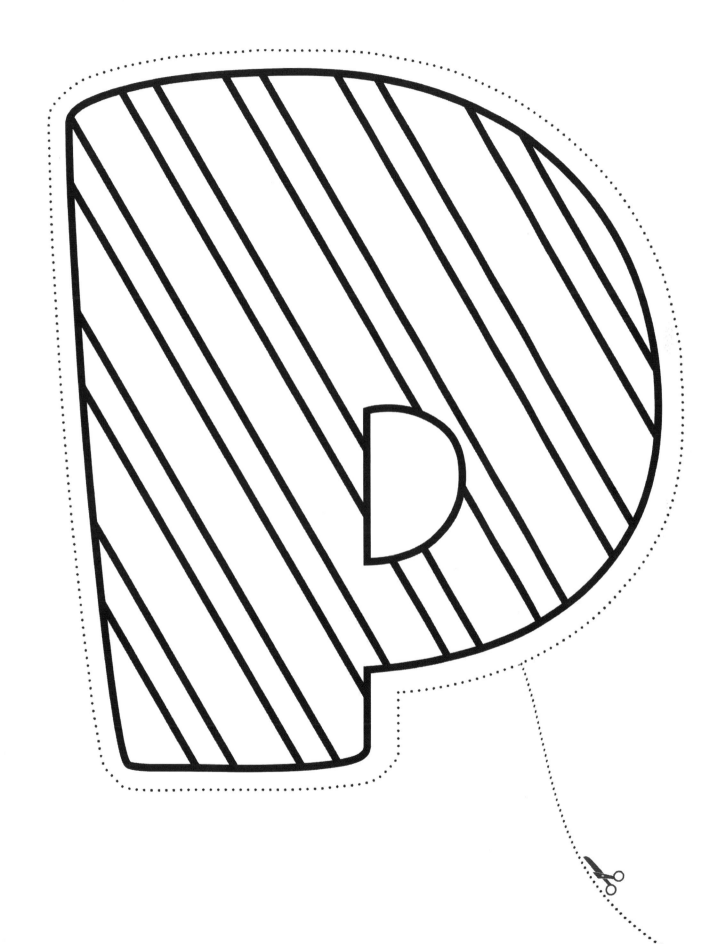

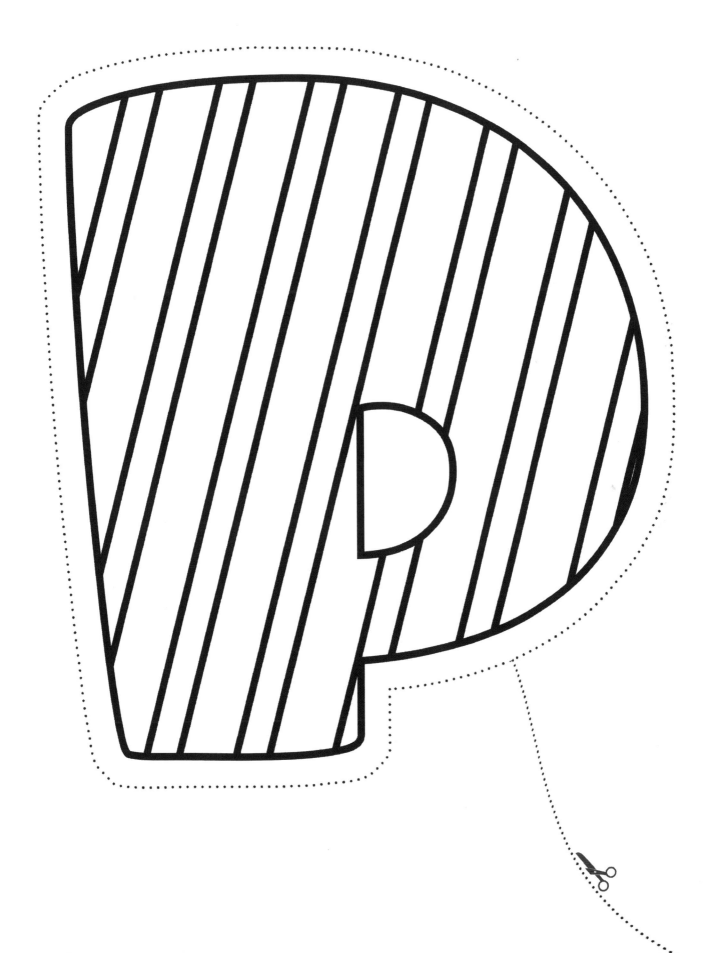

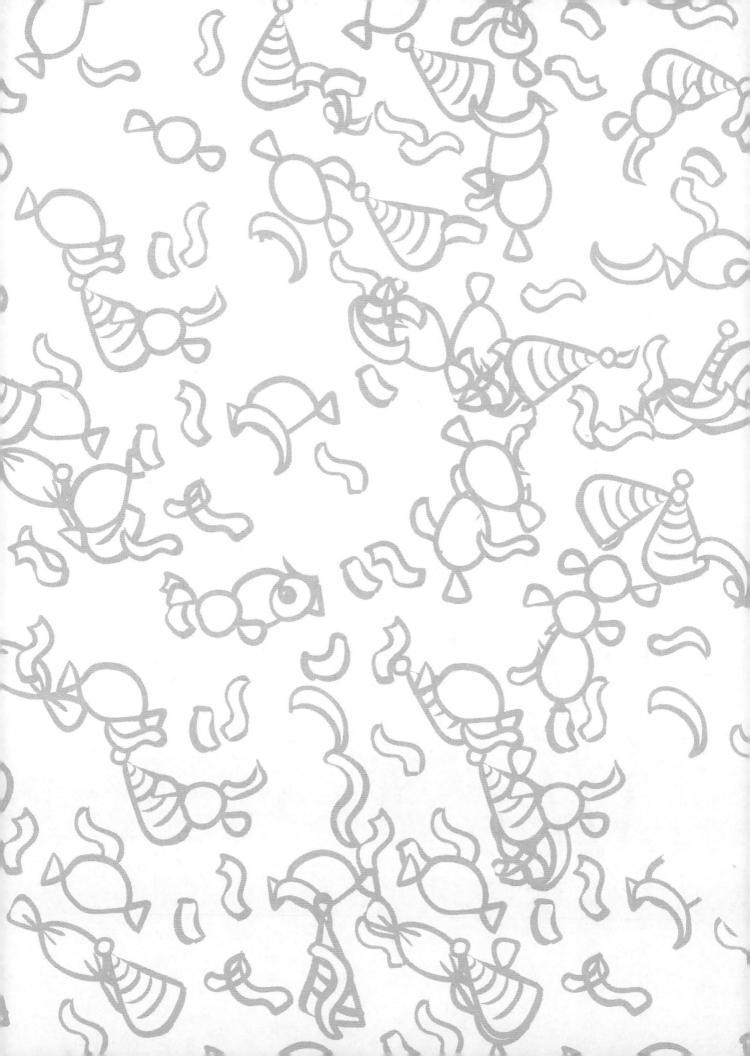

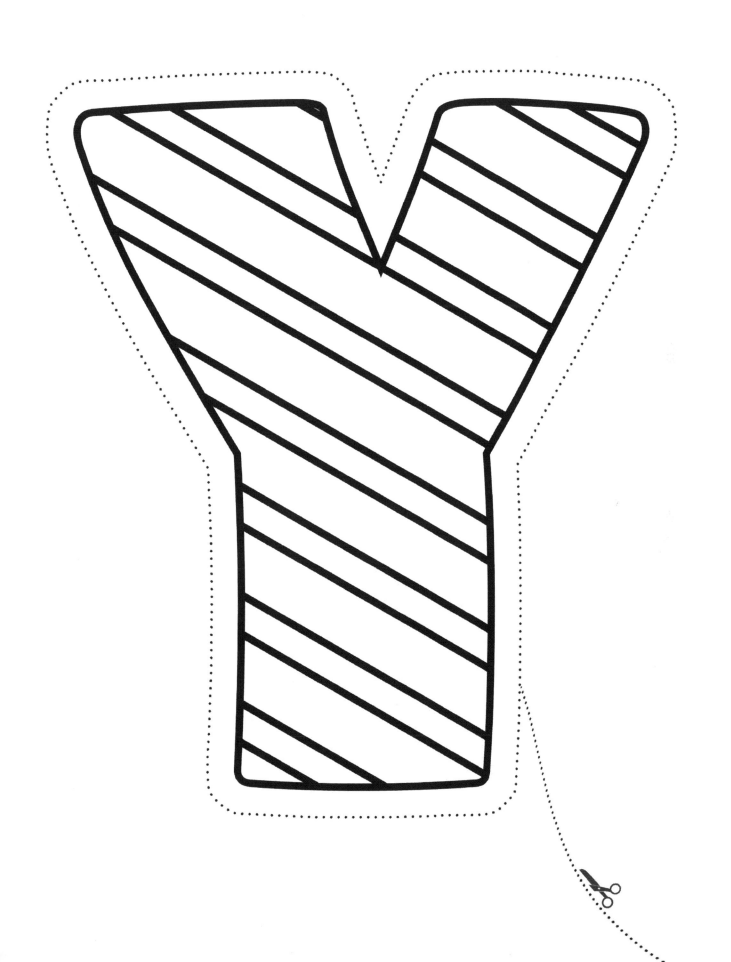

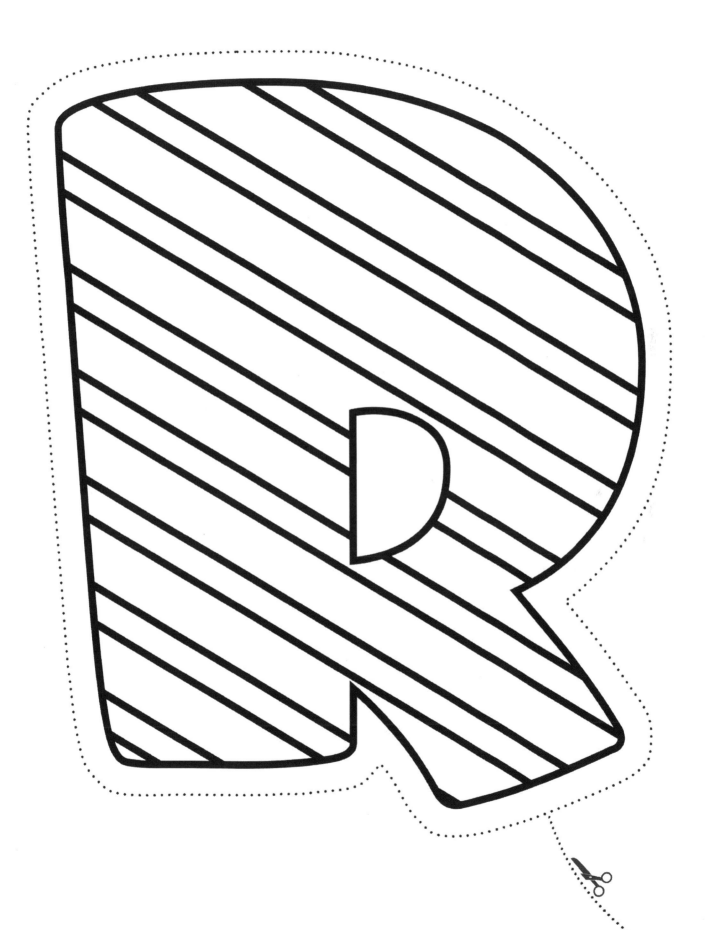

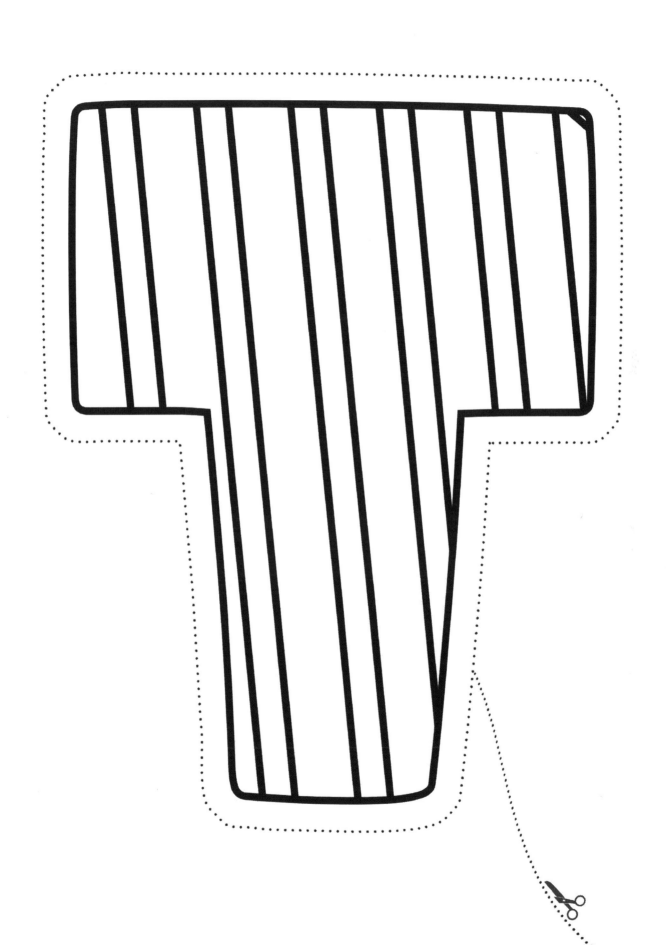

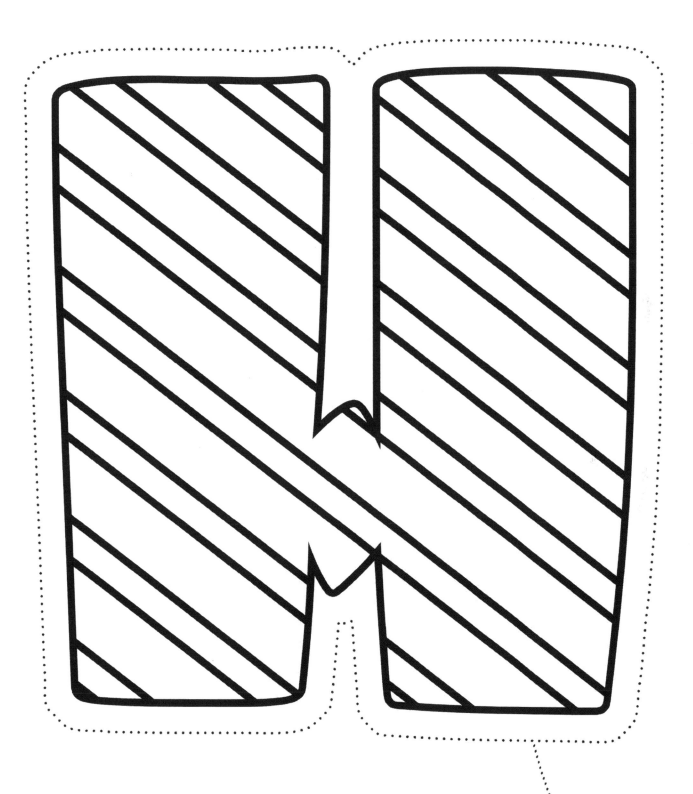

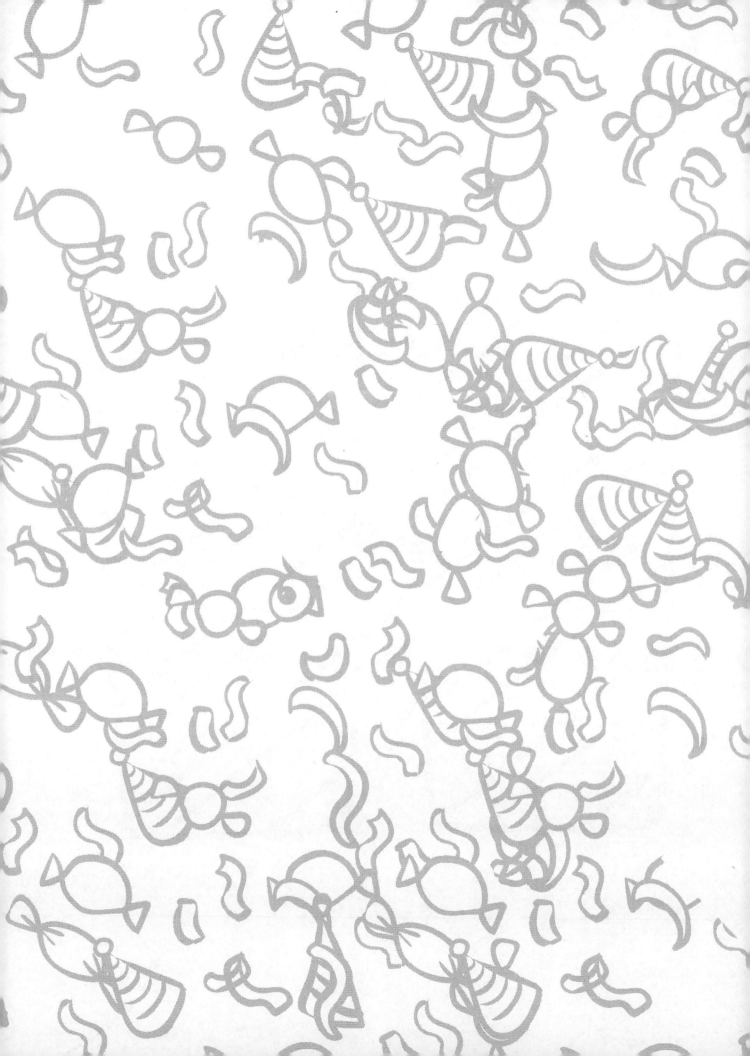

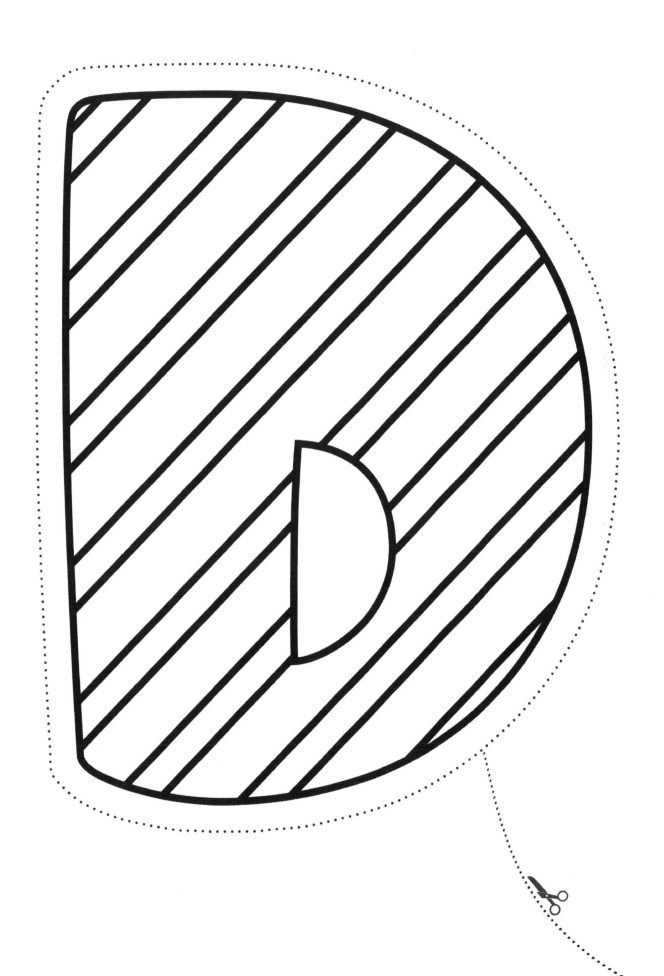

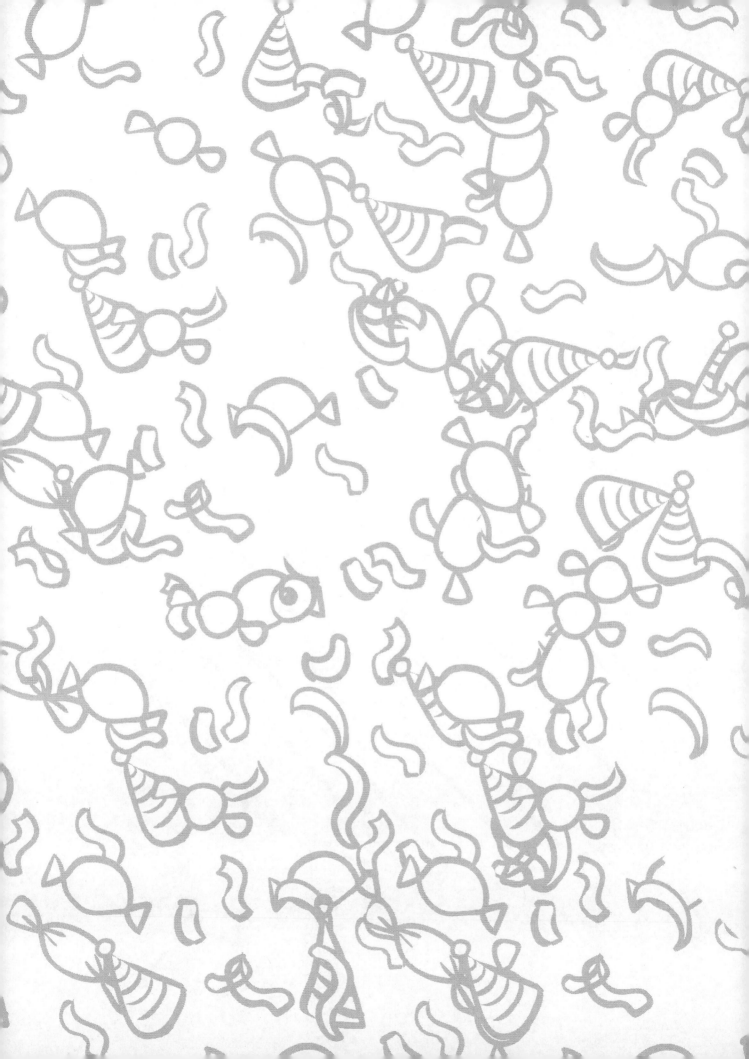

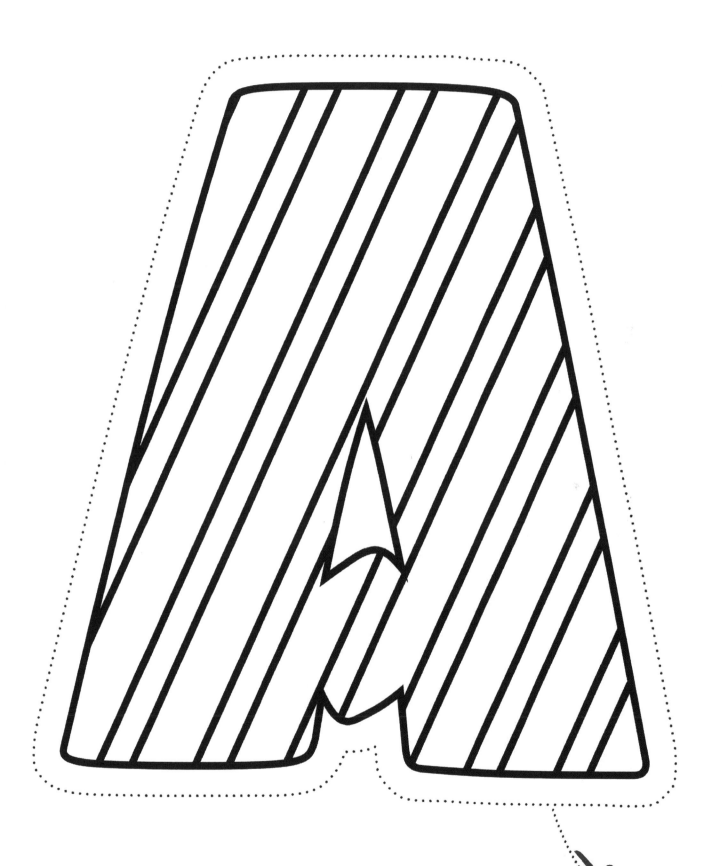

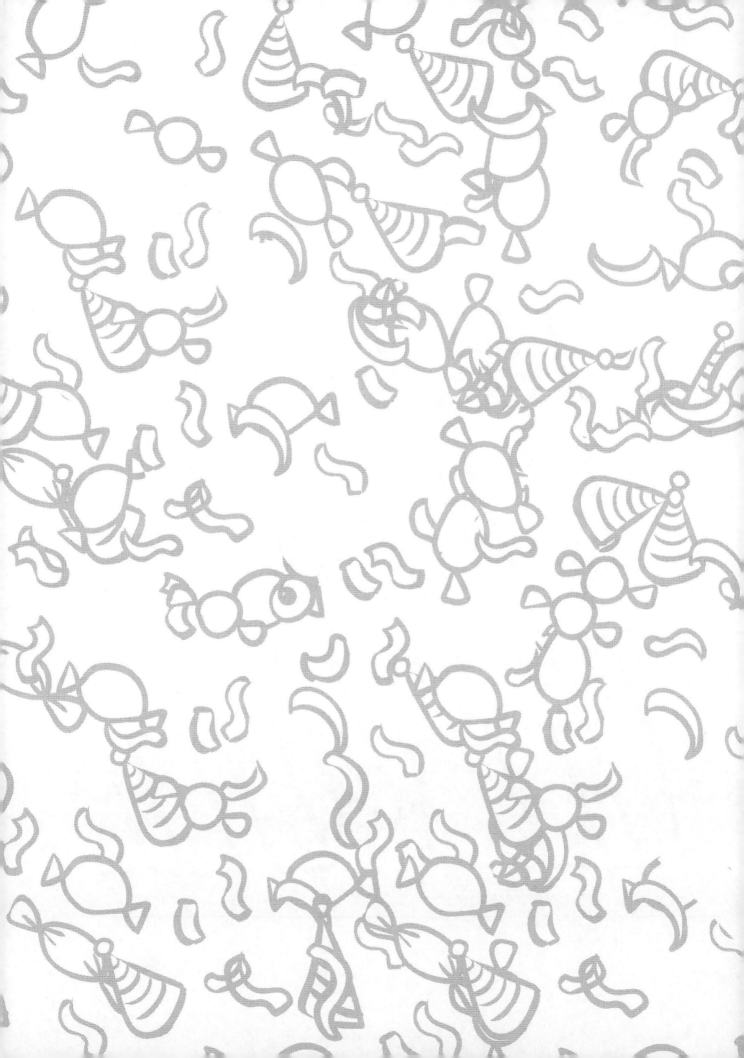

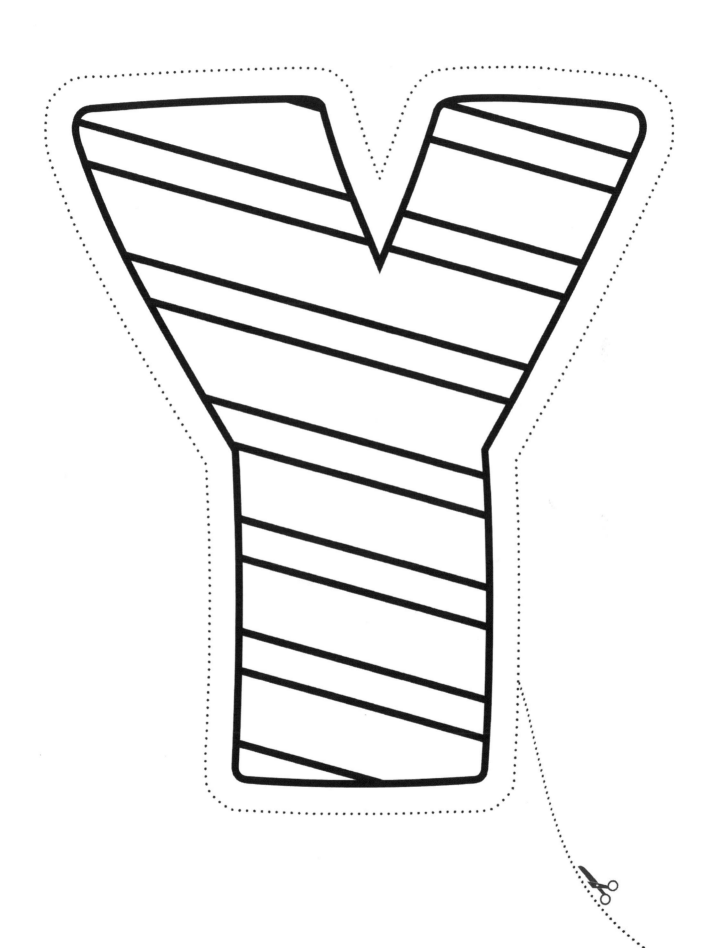

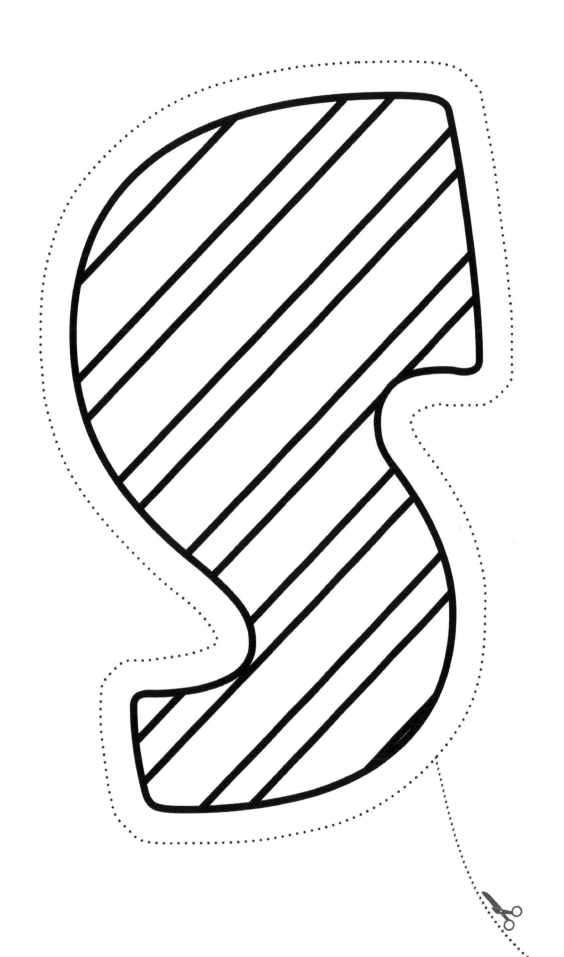

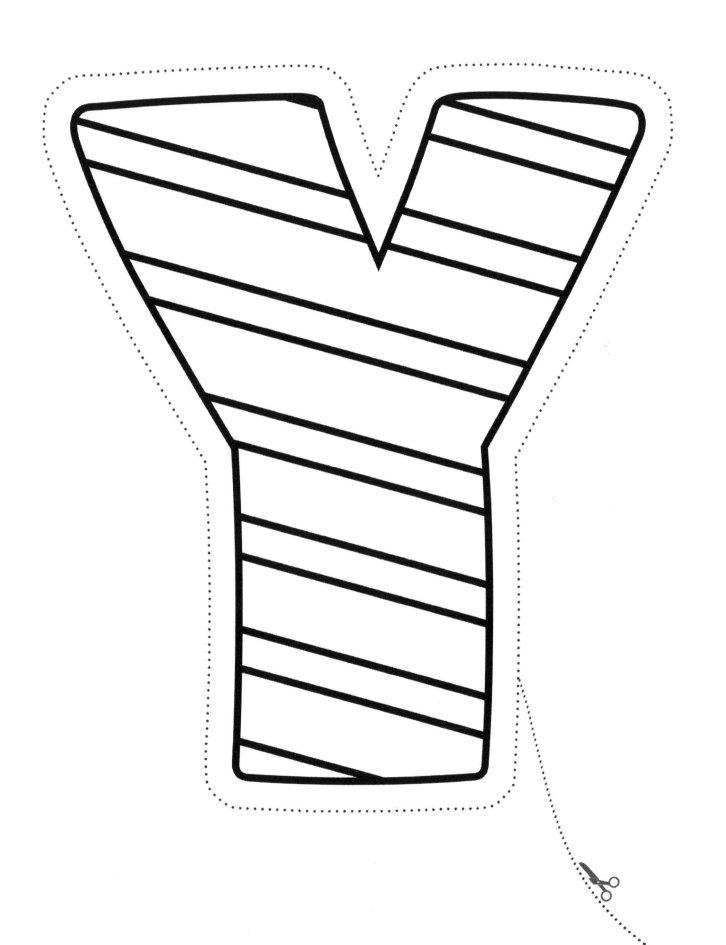

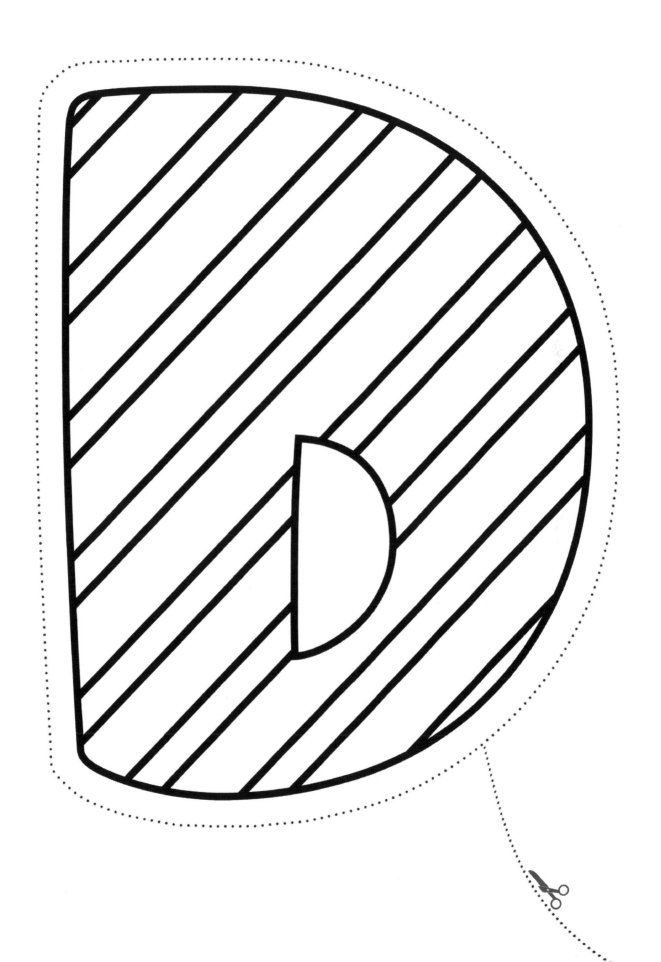

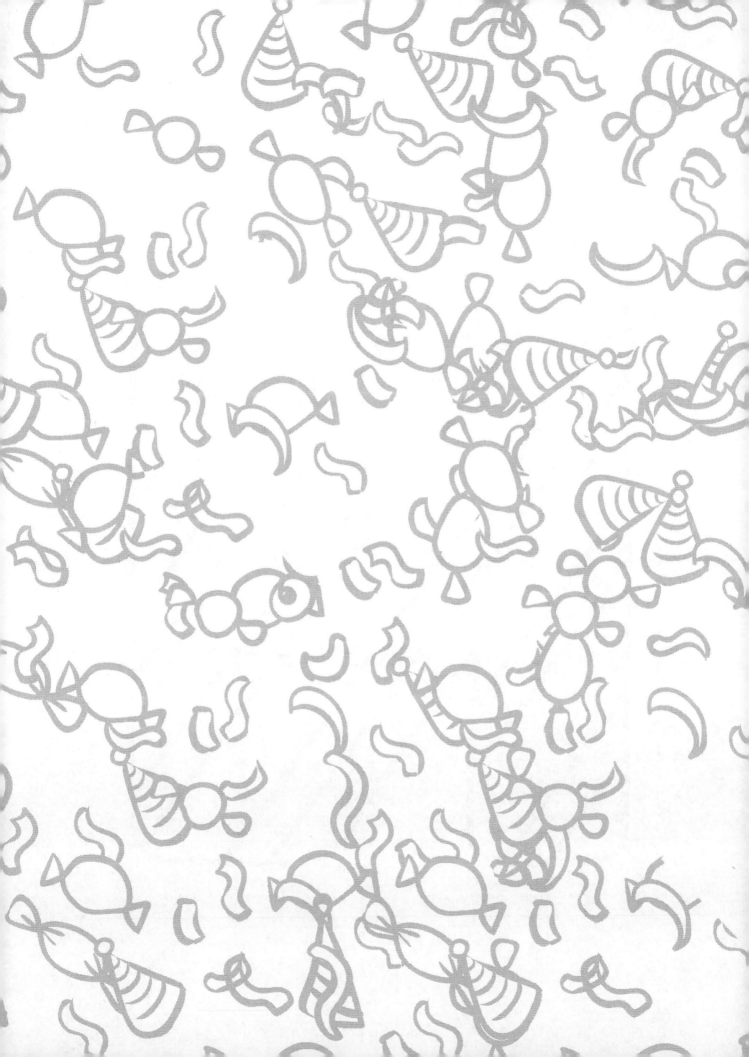

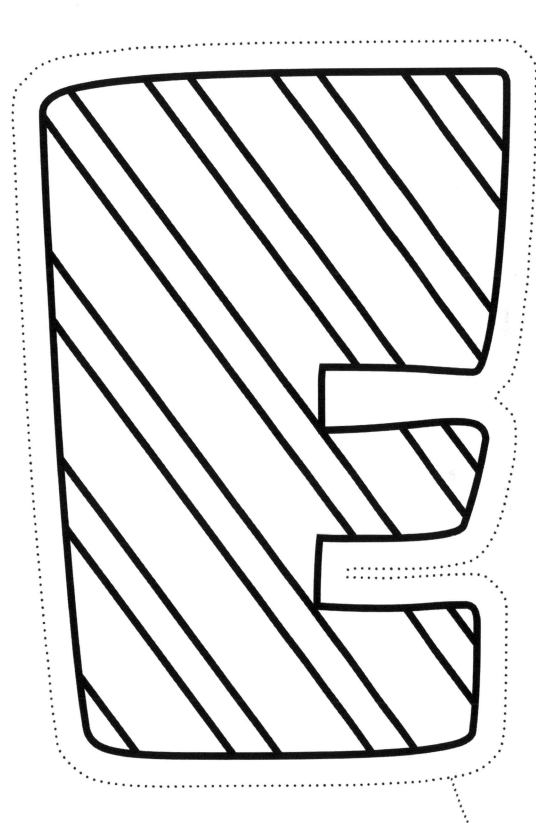

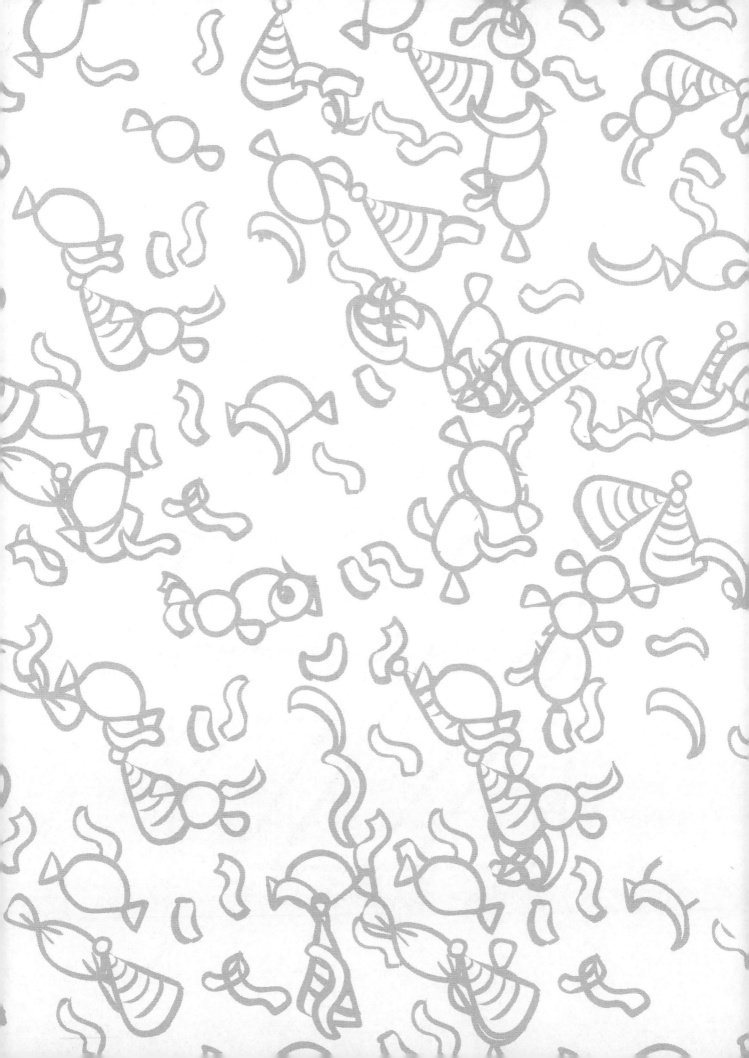

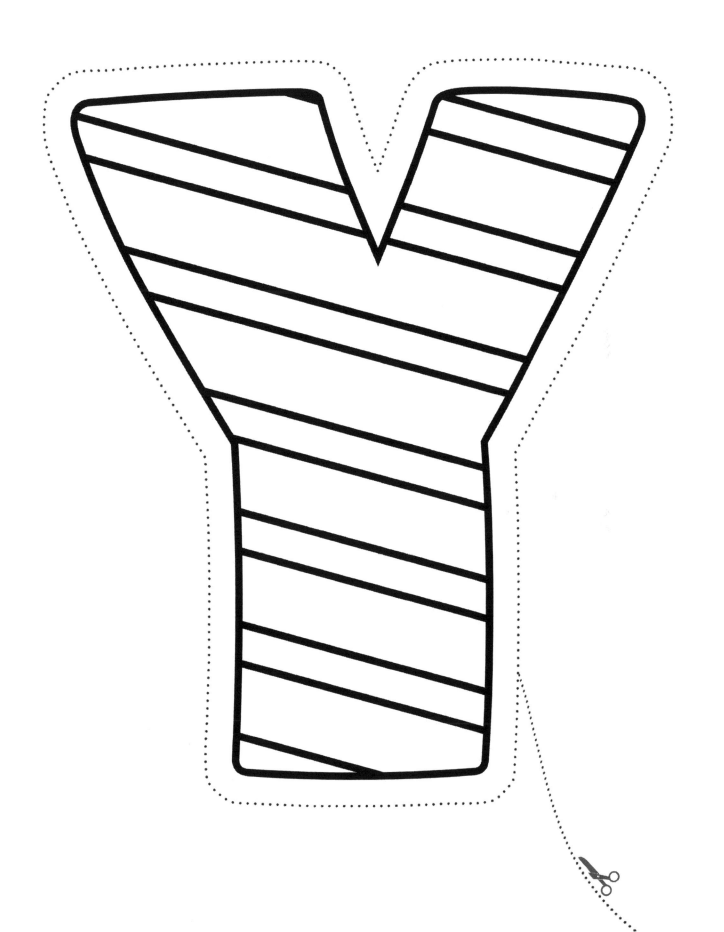

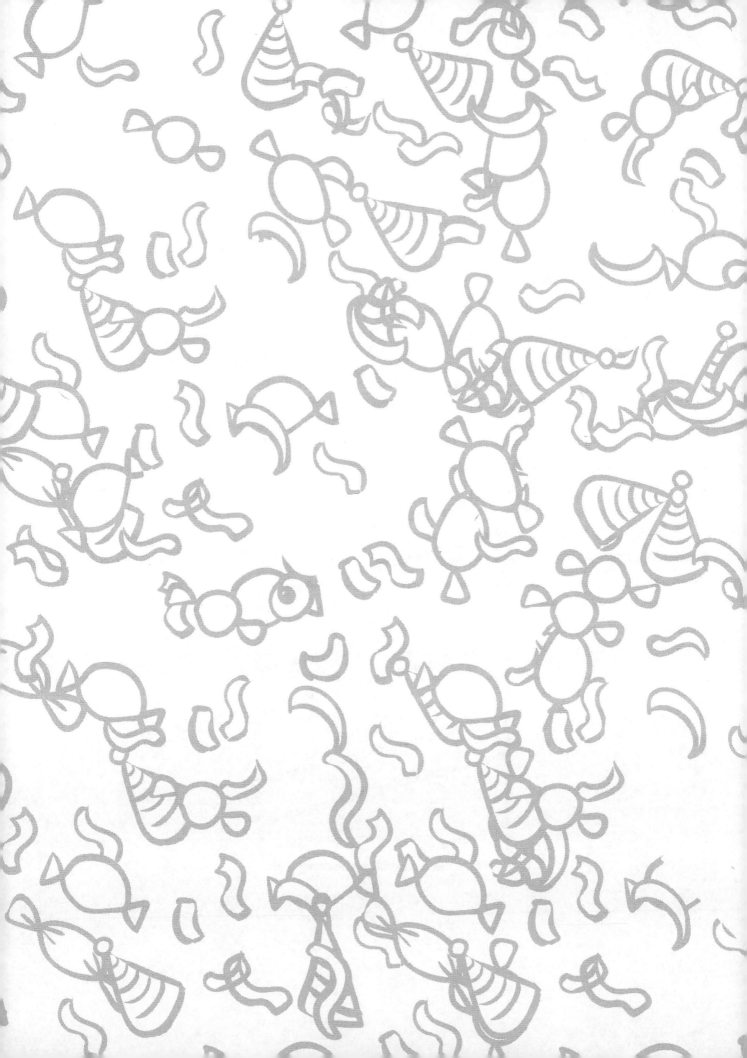

Made in United States
Orlando, FL
02 August 2022